# Wordsworth House

Cockermouth

THE NATIONAL TRUST

## Childhood in the 18th century

During the 18th century, attitudes to children changed. Theorists such as Locke and Rousseau advised parents that children should not be cosseted and restricted, as they had been in previous centuries. Instead, they should be allowed to behave naturally and to play in the open air.

Mr and Mrs Wordsworth may have adopted this approach to bringing up their children. Mrs Wordsworth seems to have been close to her children. Indeed, William later described her as 'the heart and hinge of all our learnings and our loves'. He also remembers time spent reading with his father.

In spite of the new attitude to children, by today's standards discipline was strict. A difficult child with a 'stiff and moody and violent temper', William was regularly and severely punished for bad behaviour.

# A POET'S BIRTHPLACE

*'Fair seed-time had my soul, and I grew up*
*Foster'd alike by beauty and by fear;*
*Much favour'd in my birthplace …'*

THE PRELUDE (1805)

In 1764 John Wordsworth, a 23-year-old lawyer, moved into what is now called Wordsworth House. This was a 'tied' house, which came with his job as Agent for Sir James Lowther's Cumberland estates. For nearly twenty years it served as both his office and his family home.

John and Ann Wordsworth, who married in 1766, had five children, of whom William, the future poet, was the second. Richard was born in 1768, William in 1770, Dorothy on Christmas Day 1771, John in 1772 and Christopher in 1774. For many years their home must have echoed with the sounds of lively children. In poems written later, such as *The Prelude*, William Wordsworth recalls his early childhood in Cockermouth with warmth and happiness.

This happy life came to an end in 1778, when Ann Wordsworth died, aged only 30. Dorothy was sent to live with relatives in Halifax, whilst Richard and William left to attend Hawkshead Grammar School, returning to Cockermouth only in school holidays. Only five years later, the children's lives were blighted further by the death of their father. At this point, they were forced into the care of relatives, leaving Cockermouth for ever.

Although sadly shortened, there is little doubt that William Wordsworth's early years in Cockermouth were extremely important to him. This was where he and Dorothy nurtured a devotion to the natural beauty of the Cumbrian countryside, which would inspire them for the rest of their lives.

During 2004 Wordsworth House was transformed by the National Trust in an exciting restoration project, to look as it might have when the Wordsworths lived here. Today, we hope you will get a tangible sense of what it was like to live in 18th-century Cockermouth.

*Top* The young William and Dorothy loved to play in the garden of Wordsworth House

*Left* William Wordsworth in 1798; the first reliable portrait

*Opposite* Toys in the Children's Bedroom include a jumping jack, wooden pull-along animals, building blocks, spinning tops, animals on sticks, a doll and a windmill

# A CHANGING HOUSE

## The exterior

Wordsworth House was built to impress. Certainly, a house of this size would have made quite an impact amongst the people of Cockermouth, when it was first built at the end of the 17th century. When sash-windows and a classical porch were added in the 1740s, it must have seemed even more elegant.

The front garden has been newly laid out, following archaeological research into what it might have looked like in the 18th century. The two circular flower-beds are edged with box and surrounded by local red sandstone flags. The effect is simple and formal, intended to make an impression on passers-by.

## *Origins*

In spite of an inscription above the back door claiming that this house was built by Joshua Lucock in 1745, deeds show that the first owner was William Bird in the 1690s.

## *The early 18th century*

For the first 40 years of the 18th century, the house was lived in by agents to wealthy landowners, who seem to have altered it little. This changed, however, in 1744, when Joshua Lucock bought the property (as well as pew number 26 in the church) for £350.

As Sheriff of Cumberland and a JP, Lucock was a man of some standing, which he wanted his house to reflect. During two years of improvements, he added classical decoration as well as fashionable new panelling, doors and sash-windows.

## *1764–83: John Wordsworth*

As William Wordsworth's father did not own the building (which had passed into the hands of his employer, Sir James Lowther), he may at first have contented himself with refreshing the decorations. But about 1780 he seems to have updated the fireplaces with carved overmantels.

## *The 19th century*

During the 19th century very few changes were made to Wordsworth House. It remained in the hands of the Lowther family, lived in by lawyers representing their interests – first James Clark Satterthwaite and then William Wood.

By the time the house was bought by Robinson Mitchell the younger, in 1885, it was probably in need of attention. He made improvements throughout the house and in the garden.

## *From doctor's surgery to poet's memorial*

From 1907 to 1937 the house served as home and surgery to three doctors, and there are still people in Cockermouth today who remember visiting the doctor here.

In 1937 Dr Cleveland Ellis sold Wordsworth House to Cumberland Motor Services, which intended to demolish it to make way for a bus station. Thankfully, local people formed the Wordsworth Memorial Fund, raising money to buy back the house for £1,625, before handing it to the National Trust in 1938. The doors were opened to the public for the first time on 3 June 1939.

*Above* The Scotch carpet
in the Entrance Hall was
woven following the design
of a carpet at Townend
dating from 1765

*Right* The Front Office,
where Mr Wordsworth
would have carried out his
work as Agent to Sir James
Lowther, as well as his own
private legal practice with
other clients

# A LIVING, WORKING HOME

**The Entrance Hall** ✎
With its fluted columns and impressive staircase, it was designed to make an impact on visitors. However, only the most important guests would have entered here. Most people had to use the rear entrance.

Clients or tenants waiting to see Mr Wordsworth might have been asked to sit in the Entrance Hall. The bench has been made in Cumbrian oak, copying an 18th-century north-country original.

**The Front Office** ✎
This room is shown as the domain of Mr Wordsworth. One of the smartest rooms in the house, with fine panelling and an elaborate cornice, it may well have served as the 'Front Office' mentioned in Wordsworth family papers.

*Furniture*
The mahogany desk, on loan from the Wordsworth Trust, is known to have belonged to John Wordsworth and may have been made for this room. It is dated 1766 – the year in which he married Ann Cookson. On the desk are copies of some of the letters and other documents written here by John Wordsworth.

*Prints*
After John Wordsworth's death in 1783, a notice appeared in the *Cumberland Pacquet* newspaper, advertising the sale of his belongings (illustrated on p.23). Included in the list of items for sale was 'a great Variety of valuable Prints, glassed and framed'. The prints on the walls here reflect the type of image likely to have been collected by Mr Wordsworth. Either side of the desk are portrait engravings of the reigning monarch, King George III, and Queen Charlotte. There are also two 18th-century coloured maps of Cumberland and Westmorland, including one dated 1760, which is dedicated to Sir James Lowther (right of fireplace).

**Sir James Lowther**
Sir James Lowther (1736–1802) was one of the wealthiest and most powerful men in 18th-century England. He inherited a massive fortune and vast estates, including the Whitehaven collieries, at the age of fourteen. In 1761 he married Lady Mary Stuart, whose father became Prime Minister the following year. He was made 1st Earl of Lonsdale in 1784.

Lowther's ambition was to control all ten parliamentary seats in Cumberland and Westmorland. They included Cockermouth, where Lowther spent £58,060 in 1756 acquiring a majority of the 278 burgages in the town. Ownership of these plots of land brought with it the right to nominate Cockermouth's two MPs without an election. During the second half of the 18th century, Lowther dominated the political life of the region.

*Above* Sir James Lowther was renowned for being ruthless, determined and mean. He was widely detested and feared by people in the area, earning the nickname 'the Tyrant of the North'

## The Dining Room ✎

This would have been one of the Wordsworths' best rooms, used for dinner parties and family meals on special occasions.

### Plasterwork

This is the only room in the house to have decorative plasterwork on the ceiling, which reflects its importance. The evidence of paint samples shows that most of the decoration dates from 1744–6. The fire surround was updated at the same time, although the late 18th-century decorative overmantel may have been added by the Wordsworths.

### Furnishings

The furniture, such as the mahogany Hepplewhite chairs, is typical of a middle-class Georgian dining room, as is the mid-green paint colour. There are no curtains, because soft furnishings were thought to harbour the smell of stale food.

## The Back Office ✎

John Wordsworth employed a clerk to assist him in administering Lowther's Cumberland estates. This simple room, located conveniently close to the Front Office, may have served as his office. Here, the clerk would have laboured for long hours, keeping records, copying documents and receiving tenants.

### Tools of the trade

Amongst the scattered papers are items likely to have been used every day by a clerk, such as a wax-jack (a self-snuffing candle), ink pots and bottles, quills and coins. Estate maps hang on the walls, including a reproduction of Thomas Donald's 1774 map of Cumberland (illustrated on p.19).

### An agent's life

John Wordsworth's job as Agent involved travelling around Lowther's Cumberland estates holding manor courts (which arbitrated on local disputes), collecting rents from tenants, and inspecting estate properties. He also defended his master in legal matters, and became involved in canvassing political support for him at election time. His salary was £100 a year.

Wordsworth's accounts show that he was an extremely busy man, often away from home on Lowther business and travelling long distances on horseback. A recently discovered day book has revealed that he also had his own private legal practice, which seems to have been lucrative.

*Top* John Wordsworth employed at least one clerk in the Back Office. One man, William Arnott, stayed with him for ten years, and was paid £5 per quarter

*Above* The furniture in the Back Office, including a desk and stool in elm and a pine plan chest, has been remade following 18th-century office furniture shown in pictures such as *The Cabinet Maker's Office*

*Above* The oak dresser in the Common Parlour is laden with crockery that the family would have used on a daily basis: creamware plates and jugs, pewter dishes and tankards, salt and pepper pots, and a collection of wine glasses

*Right* A recipe from Elizabeth Raffald's *Experienced English Housekeeper* (1775)

*Opposite* The Kitchen is cluttered with reproduction and antique cooking utensils, brass and copper pans, pewter plates, mixing bowls, char pots, sieves, jugs and plates, and dried herbs and hams hanging from the ceiling

*Opposite far right* Earthenware and stoneware jars, filled with grain, flour, dried fruits, herbs, and spices and sealed with chamois leather

## The Common Parlour ✎

A Common Parlour was a multi-purpose room, likely to have been used regularly by the family, and often serving as a dining room. Mrs Wordsworth may have worked in here during the day, whilst keeping an eye on the maid in the Kitchen next door.

### Furniture

As this would not have been one of the Wordsworths' best rooms, it may have housed their more old-fashioned oak furniture. In this room the collection of antique furniture includes the kind of pieces commonly found in mid-18th-century households in the north of England. The oak mule chest was made for Thomas Iredale of Cockermouth in 1737, and many of the chairs came from the Lake District.

## The Kitchen ✎

The Wordsworths' kitchen would have been at the heart of their home – a centre of activity, a source of noise, warmth and smells, and a place for the servants and children to eat. But a kitchen like this must have been a tiring environment in which to work.

This fascinating room has been recreated by food historian Peter Brears, based on evidence found in the room and examples of similar kitchens elsewhere.

### Fixtures and fittings

In Georgian times, the most important cooking methods were roasting, boiling and stewing. In this kitchen, roasting would have taken place on a spit in front of a fire burning in the cast-iron range. The spit would have been turned by a smoke-jack fitted to the chimneybreast, powered by the passage of smoke upwards through the flue. A wood-fired 'beehive' oven, fitted to the right of the range, would have been used for baking bread and cakes. The range is flanked by a boiling copper (on the right) and a charcoal stewing stove (on the left) used for making sauces.

In the corner, by the boiling copper, the sink is fitted with a draining rack. Next to it is a dresser with a 'delft rack' above, for storing plates. Opposite the fireplace, an arched recess has been fitted out as a built-in dresser – the shelves loaded with pots, pans and jars.

### Furniture

The large reproduction table in the centre of the room would have provided a surface for preparing vegetables, rolling pastry, beating eggs and stirring cake mixture. Its sycamore top could be scrubbed down at the end of the day. A replica dough trough, in which dough was mixed, fermented and left to prove before baking, stands between the windows.

*To make a rich Seed Cake.*

TAKE a Pound of Flour well dried, a Pound of Butter, a Pound of Loaf Sugar beat and sifted, eight Eggs, two Ounces of Carriway Seeds, one Nutmeg grated, and its Weight of Cinnamon; first beat your Butter to a Cream, then put in your Sugar, beat the Whites of your Eggs half an Hour, mix them with your Sugar and Butter, then beat the Yolks half an Hour, put it to the Whites, beat in your Flour, Spices, and Seeds, a little before it goes to the Oven, put it in the Hoop and bake it two Hours in a quick Oven, and let it stand two Hours.—It will take two Hours beating.

## Food and drink

The food eaten by the Wordsworth household would have been plain and substantial. Meals would have been dominated by meat, fish, pies and dairy produce. Filled suet puddings and sweet baked puddings were also popular. A variety of vegetables, grown in the garden, would have been served boiled, often covered with melted butter. Apples, rhubarb and gooseberries were eaten raw, added to tarts, or made into jams.

When cooking, it is very likely that Mrs Wordsworth and her maid worked from books such as Elizabeth Raffald's *Experienced English Housekeeper* (1775), in which they would have found recipes for 'pike boiled with a pudding in the belly', potted char (a local fish), 'calf's head surprise', herb fritters and syllabubs.

*Top* The Best Parlour
wallpaper reproduces an
English design of the
1760s. It is block-printed in
distemper on small sections
of paper – as it would have
been in the 18th century

*Above* The advertisement
listing items for sale after
John Wordsworth's death
includes 'a large and
handsome Wilton Carpet',
which was probably laid in
the Drawing Room. This
new Wilton was woven to
the design of an 18th-
century Indian carpet

*Right* The Best Parlour

*Opposite* The Drawing
Room

### The Best Parlour 🖎

In this comfortable room, overlooking the garden, Mrs Wordsworth might have worked at the spinning wheel, kept her accounts or written letters at her desk. This was a room containing some of the family's better mahogany furniture, where they could entertain close friends.

### *Furniture*

The mahogany kneehole desk has been newly made following a *c.*1760 original by the Lancaster-based firm, Gillows, which produced some of the most fashionable furniture available in the 18th century. Such an elegant small-sized desk would have been used by the lady of the house, who would have been able to lock her papers in the drawers to prevent servants from snooping at the contents!

  Two fine chairs, also made new, have

been fitted with blue check case covers over upholstery of scarlet harateen (a woollen cloth often chosen for furnishings in the 18th century), which has also been used for the curtains.

### The Wordsworth Room 🖎

This contains a settee and longcase clock owned by Wordsworth in later life.

### The Drawing Room 🖎

The grand and imposing Drawing Room was probably used only when Mr and Mrs Wordsworth were entertaining. Here they could show off their most fashionable furnishings. When not in use, the furniture would have been fitted with covers, to protect it from dust and excitable children.

### *Decoration*

Paint analysis has shown that, when the Wordsworths moved in, this room was probably painted an olive green colour, as it is now. This was the first colour applied to the panelling and carved decoration, installed in the 1740s.

### *Furniture*

The furniture – arranged for a social occasion – consists of two mahogany tripod tables and a side-table, a pair of Chippendale armchairs upholstered in fine red damask, and a child's armchair, all dating from 1750–80. The set of five early 18th-century walnut chairs with horsehair seats once belonged to the poet Robert Southey, whilst the bureau bookcase was owned by William Wordsworth (and given by his great-granddaughter).

## Entertaining

Entertaining friends and relatives was the most common form of amusement amongst middle-class families in the 18th century. As a prominent figure in Cockermouth, John Wordsworth may have regularly played host to friends and business associates. Arrangements for these occasions would have been made by his wife, anxious to provide an impressive display of food and drink.

Dinner parties, which began in mid-afternoon, were the usual form of entertainment. The meal itself was generally a substantial and lengthy affair, sometimes lasting four to five hours. During the dinner, ladies would sit at one end of the table, and gentlemen at the other, so that each group could converse easily.

After dinner, the ladies would retire to the Drawing Room to prepare tea, whilst the men raised toasts and drank more wine. Tea would be served in the Drawing Room for the entire party, who might then engage in a game of cards, or even dancing on special occasions.

*Top* The Closet wallpaper
is a replica of a 1760s
pattern

*Above* The Scotch carpet
in the Children's Bedroom
is the reverse of that in the
Entrance Hall

*Right* Mrs Wordsworth's
Bedroom, with the Closet
beyond

## THE WORDSWORTHS' BEDROOMS

*Leading directly off the landing, the best bedchamber, shown as Mrs Wordsworth's Bedroom, is a handsome panelled room with a closet. A second bedroom (Mr Wordsworth's) is approached through a connecting doorway.*

### Mrs Wordsworth's Bedroom 🖎

The room is dominated by a Chippendale-style four-poster bed, hung with white lawn linen with a floral sprig pattern. This fabric, copying an English fabric dating from 1765, is also used for the 18th-century-style 'festoon' window curtains. The mid-18th-century oak tripod table is thought to have belonged to Dorothy Wordsworth.

### Pictures

The panelled walls are decorated with three embroidered silkwork pictures, an oil portrait – *Boy with a Bird's Nest* after the English artist Thomas Hudson – and an engraving of a Scottish ballad scene (all dating from the 1760s–'70s).

### Gown

Laid out on the bed is a gown made of dark red silk taffeta which would have been worn by a woman of Mrs Wordsworth's standing. It is in the 'Polonaise' style of the 1770s.

### The Closet 🖎

The Closet, papered with a replica 1760s wallpaper and border, was used as a dressing room. The 1770s chest-of-drawers belonged to the poet Robert Southey.

### Mr Wordsworth's Bedroom 🖎
### Furniture

The bed has been newly made in the style of Gillows of Lancaster. The footposts – the only visible part of the bed frame – are African mahogany (from sustainable sources), whereas the rest is local oak. The bed-hangings and window curtains are blue harateen.

The simple arrangement of furniture around the bed includes a dressing-table (cluttered with a snuffbox, neck tie, shaving bowl and lawyer's wig), side-table and commode corner chair, which would have housed a chamber-pot.

### The Children's Bedroom 🖎

It is possible that all five Wordsworth children shared this large plain room at the back of the house. From here they would have been able to look out over their favourite playground – the garden and the banks of the River Derwent.

### Furniture

Just as happens today, the Wordsworths would have relegated their old-fashioned furniture to rooms such as the children's bedroom. The painted pine clothes press, side-table and rocking chair have been made to reflect this kind of furniture. The early 18th-century oak bed came from Lancashire. It is strung with rope, and cannot have been particularly comfortable.

Wicker cradles were popular during the Wordsworths' time, not only because they were light and airy, but also because they could be burnt easily in case of disease.

### Toys and Games

Today, most children have a vast array of exciting and colourful toys. Children in the 18th century, however, would have owned fewer, simpler toys. Most of those owned by the Wordsworth children would have been homemade, from wood or cloth. Some may have been bought from street traders at fairs and markets.

The first books written specifically for children were published in the 1740s, such as the *Little Pretty Pocket Book* by John Newbery, and soon a wide variety was available to buy. Magical fairy tales, handed down for generations, were also a common source of amusement.

*Above* The Children's Bedroom

# THE REAR GARDEN

'...*Was it for this*
*That one, the fairest of all Rivers, lov'd*
*To blend his murmurs with my Nurse's song.'*
THE PRELUDE (1805)

William Wordsworth's memories of his early life in Cockermouth are dominated by happy times spent exploring the garden. As well as being an exciting playground, the garden was also a vital source of food for the household. It has been recently replanted to show how the Wordsworth family might have used it during the 1770s.

## A changing garden

The recent changes have been made following a programme of research, looking at how the garden has altered during the last 300 years. This investigation included a geophysical survey, an archaeological dig and a study of local maps.

The basic structure of the rear garden, with a smaller kitchen garden and a raised terrace running parallel to the River Derwent, dates back to the end of the 17th century, when the house was built.

Until recently, a lawn covered the central part of the garden. However, it is thought that when the Wordsworths lived here, the rear garden may have been put to more practical use as a space for growing fruit and vegetables.

## The Terrace

Originally, the terrace would have been created as a promenade on which to take exercise and view the river. For William and Dorothy, however, it was a favourite playground – bordered by rose and privet bushes and alive with birds and butterflies. In *The Prelude* Wordsworth recalls many hours spent on the terrace and below on the banks of the river under the watchful eye of his nursemaid.

## Planting

The side borders contain mature espalier fruit trees – with traditional varieties of pears on one side and apples on the other. Enclosed by low box hedges is mixed planting of annual and perennial flowers, including nasturtiums and violas.

In the 'Physic' beds, half-standard 'Greenup Pippin' apples are underplanted with a mixture of medicinal herbs, such as cotton lavender, feverfew, tansy and marigolds, with an edging of hyssop. The top bed, linking the two 'Physic' beds, is planted with damask and musk roses, surrounded by a lavender hedge. Cut flowers grow in the bed nearest the house.

The central raised beds are planted with varieties of vegetables available in the 18th century, such as Swiss chard, French beans, spinach, fennel and black radishes. Each bed contains one main type of vegetable. These are rotated each year to improve the fertility of the soil, just as the Wordsworths' gardener might have done. Annual herbs like borage and sage are grown with the vegetables to assist pollination.

*Top* William had fond childhood memories of exploring the garden with his sister Dorothy

*Above* The 'Physic' beds are surrounded by low box hedges

*Above and left* The rear
garden is now populated
with the kinds of plants
likely to have been
available to the
Wordsworths. The
geometrical pattern of beds
is based on the evidence
of Ordnance Survey maps
and illustrations of other
18th-century town-house
gardens in Cumbria

*Turnpike Road from Penrith to Chalkbeck, and the Branch Road to Caldbeck.*

THE next Meeting of the Trustees of the said Road, is appointed to be held at the House of Mr. William Nelson, at the White Swan, in Penrith, on Tuesday the 19th Day of September next, at Eleven o'Clock in the Forenoon, at which Time the Tolls arising at the Toll Gate upon Catterlen Common will be let by Auction, to the best Bidder in the manner directed by the Act passed in the 13th Year of the Reign of his present Majesty King George the III. for the regulating of the Turnpike Roads; which Tolls produced between the 27th of June, 1774, and the 27th of June, 1775, the sum of Sixty one Pounds, above the Expences of collecting them.

Whoever happens to be the best Bidder, must at the same Time give Security, with sufficient Sureties, to the Satisfaction of the Trustees of the said Turnpike Road, for Payment of the Rent agreed for, and at such times as they shall direct.—As many of the Trustees as can conveniently, are requested to attend.

By Order of the Trustees,
WM. MONKHOUSE, Clerk.

### WALLS near Ravenglass.

TO be SOLD in Public, Together with in Parcels, at Mr. Stamper's in Ravenglass, on Friday the 15th of September next——All that Messuage and Tenement called WALLS, situated nigh Ravenglass, within the Manor of Muncaster, holden under Sir Joseph Pennington, Bart. at parcel of his said Manor, of the yearly customary finable Rent of 11. 5s. 4d. and a Twentypenny Fine certain, payable upon death and alienation.

A Purchaser of the whole to pay 20 Guineas in Hand, or 20 Guineas for each Parcel, and the Remainder of the Money as shall be agreed on the Day of Sale, and to have Possession at Candlemas.—Further Particulars may be had by inquiry of Mr. Thompson of Brankenwalt near Muncaster-Hall, or Mr. Fearat at Walls, who will shew the Premises.—A considerable Part of the Purchase Money may remain in the hands of the Purchaser, upon Mortgage of the Premises, or other satisfactory Security.

Whitehaven, August 8, 1775.
### WANTED for VIRGINIA.

TWO MASONS, single Men, who understand working in Brick as well as Stone; if acquainted with making and burning Brick the more acceptable.

Also a BLACK-SMITH, who has been accustomed to Country Work; if a married Man, without a Family, will suit best, as there is a House ready, which will accommoda e a Man and his Wife very well. It will be necessary that the Smith be able to write, as he will have occasion to enter all work done, in the Shop Book.

A WOMAN SERVANT is likewise wanted, Forty Years of Age, or upwards; who has acted as a Country House-keeper, and who is properly qualified for such a charge:

And an ELDERLY SEAMAN, qualified for the Care of a Ferry.

No Persons will be treated with, but such as can produce good Characters from People of Probity; and Articles for

### TALLENTIRE.

TO BE SOLD, in Public Sale, to the best Bidder, on Tuesday the 26th Day of September next, at the GLOBE-INN, in Cockermouth, in the County of Cumberland, between the Hours of three and six o'Clock in the Afternoon, according to such Conditions as shall be then and there produced (if not sold before by private Contract, of which timely notice will be given)

The Lordship or Manor of TALLENTIRE, in the County of Cumberland, with the Demesne Lands; containing 400 Acres, or thereabouts, of rich Meadow and Pasture Ground, with a Water-Corn-Mill, and all the Mines and Royalties within and under the same; together with the Mansion-house of Tallentire-hall, Garden, Hot and Green-houses, Stables, Barns, Dog-kennel and other Out-offices. Also the Corn Tythes of the Manor of Tallentire, supposed to contain 1200 Acres. This Estate pays Modus's in lieu of Hay and all other small Tythes, and is intitled to an unlimited right of Common on Row, Gilcrux, and Tallentire Commons, and is Toll free in all the Market Towns in Cumberland. There is plenty of Limestone upon the Premises, and is supposed to have both Coal and Copper within the Lordship.

——The whole of said Premises (except one Field of 14 Acres) lie all within a Ring-fence, and are situated within 3 Miles of the Sea, 3 of Cockermouth, 13 of Whitehaven, 3 of Mary-Port, and 4 of Allonby, in a fine sporting Country where there is plenty of Game.

Part of the Purchase Money will be continued in the Purchaser's Hand if required.

For further Particulars enquire of Mr. Hendry Hopper in Durham; Mr. Darnton, No. 84, Aldgate, London; Mr. Rudd, Attorney at Law, in Cockermouth; Mr. Evening, of Embleton, near Cockermouth; or of Mr. Bacon of Tallentire, who will shew the Premises.

N. B. If the above Estate is not Sold, it will be Let on the 27th Day of September, at the GLOBE, in Cockermouth aforesaid, between the Hours of 3 and 6 o'Clock in the Afternoon, in one or two Farms, for the term of 6 or 9 Years; and any Person or Persons willing to take the same are requested to deliver in their Proposals in writing.

### NOTICE.

WHEREAS the Game within the Barony and Manor of Wigton, the Manor and Forest of Westward and the Parks therein, the Manor of Caldbeck, Upton and Underfell, and the Manor of Bolton, all in the County of Cumberland, the Property of the Right Hon. George Earl of Egremont, has of late Years been greatly destroyed by Persons unqualified so to destroy the same:—It is therefore hoped that no Gentlemen will hunt, shoot, or otherwise destroy any of the Game in any of the aforesaid Manors the ensuing Season, without Leave of the Game-keeper hereafter named, first had and obtained for that Purpose.

And this public Notice is hereby given to all unqualified Persons, that if they shall presume to hunt, course, shoot, take, kill, or otherwise destroy any Hare, Partridge, Groose, or other Game in any of the Grounds, Woods, Commons, or Wastes, within the said Manors, they will be prosecuted to the utmost Rigour of the Law, by John Briseo of Crofton Hall, Esq. who is duly appointed and appointed Game-keeper under

### LONDON.

Saturday morning, at six o'clock, a messenger was dispatched from the Admiralty to the Commissioner at Woolwich, to hasten the riggers, &c. about the ships destined for foreign service.

We hear from Gibraltar, that the harbour has just been fortified by a very large swinging boom and chain, very strongly cramped with iron of several ton weight, capable of resisting the shock of any ship of the greatest force.

Concessions of a most shameful nature, we hear have been offered to be made to two foreign Courts, if they would agree to let their Ministers remain here till after the meeting of parliament.

By a letter from Bolton, dated the 9th of July, to a merchant of this city, which was received on Friday, we are assured that all there was peaceable and quiet, and that the next ship which would sail for England with dispatches from General Gage, would certainly bring an account of a reconciliation between the Provincials and the King's troops.

Friday cloathing for 12,000 men were shipped at the Tower on board a transport, to be sent to the army in America, at the same time 50 drummers and fifers embarked, having been drafted out of the several regiments for that purpose.

Most of the private men of the Provincials who fell on the 17th of June last, had in their pockets one or more six shilling notes payable by the Congress, and a hymn book.

It must give great pleasure to all lovers of their country to find that the late severe battle was fought between the east end of the Poultry and the top of Cornhill, i. e. it was an engagement between the Bulls and Bears of that part of the world.

According to the last letters from Spain, the whole fleet of that nation hath, after its unfortunate expedition against the Algerines, returned to Carthagena.

General Gage is certainly coming home, for the purpose of being here during the winter, to offer his advice, and enable Administration to know what preparations are proper to make against the ensuing spring, when he is to return again. It is also said that he is in possession of some papers that will rise in judgement against those honest patriotic gentlemen who have all along been distinguishing themselves as a set of daring rebels. Reflecting on this, and other circumstances, we may naturally expect that the ensuing winter will furnish historians with matter as extraordinary as any now to be found in the History of England. *Morn. Chron.*

The Grand Jury at Maidstone consisted of 25, out of which number 15 were for finding the indictment against the shiprights, and 10 against it.

The Barbadoes packet, ——— from Philadelphia, is arrived at Bristol in thirty two days. Governor Penn is come over express in the above ship, by desire of the Congress. They left Philadelphia the

### TUESDAY, August 8.

Orders have lately been given by Governme two frigates to sail immediately for Cape Finest Cape Orrugal, to watch the motions of the and Spaniards, and four companies of the Roy of Artillery at Woolwich, to embark for with proper stores

The last parliament of George Second, the first Parliament of George the Third, to Americans the two sums following:
31st of March 1760. For a proper compensation to the North Americans, as his Majesty shall think they merit £ 20
20th of Jan. 1761. To compensate the Americans in their expences, levies, cloathing, &c. 20

A lover of true patriotism would be glad to from some of the friends of Mr. Fox, if the p of 1800l. per ann. said to be granted to him in his Clerkship of the Pells in Ireland, be charg the Pension List of that kingdom? and if it true, but it is to be paid out of the Civil List R here, what services are they which Mr. Jenkins rendered to this country, that entitle him to reward.

An act of general forfeiture is expected to p beginning of next session of Parliament agai landed proprietors, now or hereafter in arms provinces of New-England; and their lands ar parcell'd out among the officers and soldiers employed in the conquest. This necessary will inevitably prevent all future disturbances in rica, especially as the form of government in refractory provinces is to be altogether changed

We are informed from good authority, th military operations will be confined to the provin New England; these being compleatly reduce serve as an example to the other Colonies, wh submit themselves accordingly.

Lord Chatham is so exceedingly ill as to be p hopes of recovery.

By letters received yesterday from Madrid, f way of Paris, we are informed that upwards of thousand Spaniards were actually killed on th the late engagement before the town of Algiers

By a private letter from Nantucket there is a that five Dutch vessels had landed near that 10,000 muskets, and a large quantity of powd bullets, for the use of the Provincial army, an which they received cash immediately.

The prisoners taken after the 17th of June British troops, at Bolton, have to a man declar the most solemn manner, that they never hear General Gage's proclamation.——So attenti the rebels to conceal whatever concerns the inter their country.

*From Bradford's Pennsylvania Journal.*

# COCKERMOUTH IN THE 18TH CENTURY

The Wordsworth children grew up in a small but flourishing town. Thriving on industry, Cockermouth was a centre of business and social activity, serving not only the townsfolk, but also those living in surrounding villages.

Hutchinson's *History of Cumberland* (1797) describes Cockermouth as a 'well-traded market town' with a population of 3,000. Its situation was considered to be good and healthy, although the town was apparently prone to 'fogs in the evenings'. Most activity took place on two adjoining streets – Main Street and Market Place. The latter was home to the Moot Hall and the Market House, both thought to be 'dirty and unwholesome' and since demolished. In contrast, the long and wide Main Street was 'spacious, open and well-built'. During the 18th century, as the town flourished, many new houses were built which still stand.

## Trade and industry

A trade directory of 1784 refers to Cockermouth's 'excellent situation for trade and manufactories ... having a constant and plentiful supply of water ... several valuable coal-mines, and three sea-ports, all within the small distance of 15 miles'. The most important industry was textiles, in particular the production of linen and shalloon (a coarse woollen cloth for which Cockermouth was well known). About 100 people were involved in making hats, and a further 50 in the leather trade. Although operating on a small scale, these industries must have generated activity, noise and indeed smells,

which pervaded the town. The preparation of animal hides in tanneries, for example, was a dirty and foul-smelling job, involving quantities of urine and excrement. One such tannery stood only yards upstream from the Wordsworths' house!

## Markets and fairs

Life in Cockermouth was shaped by a succession of markets and fairs. The weekly market took place on Mondays, and the cattle market on alternate Wednesdays, on Main Street. The biggest events were the hiring fairs, staged twice a year at Whitsun and Martinmas (November). Here farmers and other employers could find servants for the coming months. Amongst the servants, they were occasions for widespread merry-making, drinking, flirting and profligacy!

## Shops

The town had a wide variety of shops and tradesmen, from chandlers to coopers. More than 20 inns provided food, drink and rooms, as well as meeting places for farmers and other tradesmen.

Cockermouth was said to have 'a countenance of opulence'. But that was by the standards of the 1770s, when muddy roads, dirty water, wandering livestock and sewage-filled rivers were the norm.

*Above* Detail of Thomas Donald's 1774 map showing the centre of Cockermouth. Wordsworth House is marked in red

*Opposite The Cumberland Pacquet* reveals much about 18th-century life in Cockermouth

# DAILY LIFE IN THE WORDSWORTHS' HOME

The Wordsworths were a middle-class family, living in a grand and spacious house. Relative to most other people in Cockermouth, they appear to have led a comfortable existence.

### Organising the housework

As mistress of the house, the young Ann Wordsworth would have overseen the running of the household. She probably relied for advice on such household manuals as Martha Bradley's *British Housewife* and *The Servant's Directory* by Hannah Glasse, which provided encyclopaedic instruction in successful housekeeping.

### The Wordsworths' servants

The Wordsworths employed a modest, but standard, range of servants, including a maid-of-all-work, a manservant, a nurse to care for the children, and a 'jobbing' gardener.

The lot of the maid-of-all-work was by far the hardest, with most of the housekeeping chores falling to her. Records show that one girl, Amy, worked for the family for some time. Starting the day early, she would have cleaned grates, laid fires, emptied chamber-pots, washed floors, brushed carpets, swept floors, dusted and tidied rooms, and aired and made beds. In addition, she would have cooked and prepared meals and probably washed up afterwards. At least one day of her week would have been devoted to laundering the family's dirty linen.

By comparison, the manservant had far less to do. Despite this, Mr Wordsworth's accounts show that he had difficulty filling this position, recording payments to a succession of troublesome individuals, one of whom appears to have robbed him. Nevertheless, the manservant was probably trusted with jobs requiring more skill, such as cleaning chandeliers or silver plate. He may also have cleaned the stables and looked after his master's horses. In the afternoon he would have changed into his livery, to act as footman to his master.

### Servicing the home

The Wordsworths' house would have been lit by candles, probably arranged by the manservant. As candles were expensive and burnt quickly, they were lit only when a room was in use. Tallow candles (made from rendered animal fat) would have been used most frequently, even though they smelt unpleasant. Wax candles were reserved for special occasions.

**'Apt to take liberties'**
In *The Complete Servant
Maid* (1770) by Anne
Barker, maids are advised
to be circumspect in their
behaviour towards male
servants: *'As they have in
general little to do, they
are for the most part very
saucy and pert where they dare,
and are apt to take liberties
on the least encouragement.'*

*Above* An 18th-century
kitchen, illustrated in
Martha Bradley's *The British
Housewife* (1756)

### A childhood revisited

In restoring Wordsworth House, the aim has been to give a glimpse into the childhood years of William Wordsworth. The result, achieved after four years of research and planning, is the work not only of National Trust staff, but also of skilled craftspeople, conservators and historians.

*Right* Much of the furniture has been specially remade following historic patterns by Peter Hall & Son of Staveley near Kendal

*Opposite* This advertisement, which appeared in *The Cumberland Pacquet*, lists some of the items we know to have once been in Wordsworth House

# RESTORING WORDSWORTH HOUSE

## Research

Until recently, very little was known about Wordsworth House or the people who once lived here. Before any changes could be made, this had to be rectified, through a programme of in-depth research. Architectural historians were called in to determine how the house had changed over the centuries, whilst census and other records were examined at local record offices to trace past occupants.

The household accounts (at Dove Cottage, Grasmere) provided clear information about the Wordsworths' way of life, such as who they employed as servants, where they shopped and what they bought. The local newspaper, *The Cumberland Pacquet*, revealed fascinating facts about life in 1770s Cockermouth, and a study of inventories began to show how the Wordsworths might have furnished their house.

## Decoration

Paint analysts provided an insight into how the Wordsworths might have decorated their house, by examining samples of paint from almost every wall surface. Today, the paint colours in most rooms reflect the results of this investigation. The types of paint used (such as casein distempers) were chosen to give the finish and texture characteristic of an 18th-century home.

## Furnishings

A house becomes a home only once it is full of the belongings of the people who live there. The challenge at Wordsworth House has been to find pieces likely to have been owned by families of middling status like the Wordsworths, and, where possible originating from Cumbria. Today, the 'best' rooms (at the front of the house) have been furnished with antiques dating from the mid- to late 18th century, collected over several years.

Furnishings for the informal 'hands-on' rooms have been made by specialist crafts-people and conservators, replicating 18th-century examples. Great efforts have been made to use traditional techniques and materials, so that the finished products look and feel as they did in the 1770s. Replica items include furniture crafted by cabinet-makers and utensils forged by blacksmiths.

**As good as new**
Many of the replica items seem unexpectedly new and brightly coloured. This is because the aim throughout has been to present the house as it was lived in by the Wordsworths – when many things around them would have been new.

HOUSEHOLD FURNITURE for SALE.
Cockermouth, April 17, 1784.
THE Sale of the valuable Household Goods & Furniture, late of Mr. JOHN WORDSWORTH, of Cockermouth, will begin on Wednesday the 5th Day of May next, at Ten o'Clock in the Forenoon, and continue till the Whole be Sold: the same confist of Plate, China, very good Beds, Bed and Table Linen, Mahogany Bed Stocks, Tables and Chairs, handsome oval and square Looking Glaffes, a large and handsome Wilton Carpet, a great Variety of valuable Prints, glaffed and framed, and all other useful Household Utenfils.

The Housekeeper will shew the Goods to any Perfon desirous to fee them, before the Sale.

All Perfons who ftood indebted to the late Mr. John Wordfworth, at the Time of his Deceafe, are required to pay their refpective Debts immediately to the Administrators, or to Mr. RICHARD WORDSWORTH, Attorney at Law, at Branthwaite, near Whitehaven. (16)

# INSPIRING THE POET

*Below* Crummock Water in the Buttermere valley. In later life, Wordsworth's passion for the Cumbrian countryside would inspire not only his poetry, but also a fierce commitment to protect the Lake District from inappropriate development – a philosophy at the heart of the National Trust's work in the area today

*'The Child is father of the Man.'*
TO A RAINBOW

Although William was just thirteen when his father died, five years after his mother, he remembers his parents with strong affection. Of his mother he recalls tenderness, piety and wisdom. From his father he learnt an appreciation of literature – a love for what he later referred to as his 'golden store of books'.

The death of Mr and Mrs Wordsworth left their children 'destitute, and as we might Trooping together'. Their situation worsened when Sir James Lowther refused to pay them £4,625 owed to their father in unpaid expenses (£250,000 today). This dispute, centring on Lowther's claim that he had never agreed to pay expenses to John Wordsworth, dominated their lives for the next twenty years, and would be resolved only by Lowther's successor.

Although the children's life in Cockermouth ended in grief, William's memories of his time there are uniformly happy. During these early years, William developed a cherished bond with his sister, and a love of the Cumbrian countryside – both providing him with a lifelong source of inspiration.

*'Oh! Pleasant, pleasant were the days,*
*The time, when in our childish plays,*
*My sister Emmeline and I*
*Together chased the butterfly.'*
TO A BUTTERFLY